To the Marrow

Poems by Diana Cole

Cyberwit.net
HIG 45 Kaushambi Kunj, Kalindipuram
Allahabad - 211011 (U.P.) India
http://www.cyberwit.net
Tel: +(91) 9415091004
E-mail: info@cyberwit.net

Acknowledgments

Many thanks to the publications in which these poems first appeared, sometimes in earlier versions, and sometimes with different titles:

Blackwidow's Web of Poetry: "Beached Whales"

Off the Coast: "Outside In," "Nothing in Excess, Everything"

Spillway: "Muse"

The Aurorean: "A Charles River Tango"

Tar Poetry Review: "Time Piece"

Split Rock Review: "Night Fishing When Cod Were Still Running," "Nest"

Muddy River Poetry Review: "Nik Wallenda Walks a Wire Across Niagara Falls"

Blueline: "Loosestrife", "Cascade Link"

Tipton Poetry Journal: "Life Is Up"

Though I Walk, music composition by Thomas Stumpf

performed in New York City to an earlier version of "A Grave Imagine"

Gyroscope Review: "After an Early Snow"

To the Marrow was originally published in the United States

under the title *Songs by Heart by Iris Press*

I would like to thank those fellow poets and friends who have read my poems with candor and enthusiasm.

Three poetry groups have not only offered companionship and feedback but many festive gatherings with snacks and laughs. Thank you to the Black Oak Poets, my long-time readers and friends, Ocean State Poets for your inspiration to extend the reach of poetry into the community, and lastly the Poetry Loft for your critiques and especially for the manuscript conference that helped prepare this book.

I also want to acknowledge the insights and guidance of teachers who have been a part of my writing adventure, in particular, Brad Clompus and Tom Daley. A special thanks to PoemWorks: The Workshop for Publishing Poets—for all the poets at the "table" and for the invaluable teaching of Barbara Helfgott-Hyett. It is indeed good to be rigorous with one's poems in the company of loving people.

For Mark Wholey

Contents

Live the questions now. Perhaps then, someday far in the future,
you will gradually, without even noticing it, live your way into the answer.
                                        —Rainer Maria Rilke

Outside In

I go beyond the subject
            — Andrew Wyeth

I am outside looking in
a window to another window
looking out. I see
the glass, its fragile boundary.
My eyes pass through
to a slope so reiterated with yellow
as to be almost wasteful.

Within, dark discloses a room.
Sun ignites the geranium
on the sill. It wants this red
back in the purple shade under the maple.
But this is my flower!
I watered it, bud to blossom.
What other proof do I need of this world?

The geranium leans toward the sun,
its red blouse already loosened.

Conversing with Heisenberg

This much I know.
I am here at Long Beach
and according to my watch
it's 2:30 pm on Tuesday, June 15th,
my towel damp where I sit.

Clouds thicken, clouds burn apart.
Should I put on or throw off a sweater,
stay put or get going?
In the time it takes to eat a peach
I would rather have a plum.

So why decide what I'm going to do,
if I will leave my marriage?
When it rains I'll run quickly.
This much I know for certain.
But not where.

Up from the River

A heron walks across the yard,
dusky blue against a milk-white sky.
The neck extends and retracts
as each twig leg folds back,
reaches forward. Her toes curl,
splay, each step weighed
so as not to alarm a blade of grass.

She freezes, a soft shiver
in the tail feathers before that fist
of a torso, that flexed neck
all muscle, lowers, lunges
and a vole yanked from its burrow
twists and shakes to be free
in a shudder of dust.

Clamping down harder
the heron paces,
lets the small body exhaust itself.
Only then does the beak let go
grabbing the dazed vole
before it hits the ground.
In one swoop positions it
head first.

The river keeps on, insisting
everything to God is good
and I must swallow injustice whole.

Night Fishing When Cod Were Still Running

I drop my pail and fishing gear,
drive a spike deep into sand,
work a sea worm onto the barb.
The cod are running.
Dozens of poles lean out,
a fleet of lines pulled taut beyond the breakers.
Waves at the shoreline *hush, hush.*

The sea's sudden quivering
sets my rod jigging
my spool spinning.
Cod lift into air
flail
fall back.
I reel them in
eager to dislodge the hook
rebait
cast back into the game.

There are no throwbacks,
no chance of losing.
I bring one in
smash its head under my boot,
a brusque
but kinder death,
over what it takes
to drown in air.

This is how beauty is
without censure,
exposing the glassy shore
silvered strands stabbing through dark
the long tremolo of the reel
a flash of scales
black eyes sequined by the moon —
the wrestle, the thrash
the thud into white buckets
of fish after fish.

Beached Whales

Mortality weighs heavily on me.

— John Keats

Shoulder to shoulder
they call and call to cry,
slide onto the sand,
slack and massive,
their sleek assurance
withering in air.

With our pails
we splash and douse,
the sun pushing back.
We don't rest,
soaking burlap to wrap
blistered skin, streaming

water over their backs,
keeping airways clear.
Even as motionless hulks mount
we push to prod
each body into buoyancy,
beseech the tide to rise.

The Vine Dangles Its Multitude

of plump tomatoes in sun-drenched
musk. Wet soil clings to carrots
smelling of earth and twilight.
Green onions, chicory and dill
savory on my fingers. Everything

is dying. Potatoes wait inside
a drawer — a blackness without water.
Their eyes already in their mouths,
they grope pale arms upward
through dark distrust. I must

get to work with the knife.
The stove is lit. Water boils
starch from spinach, slips skin
from tomatoes. Quartered
beets sweat ruby drops.

Loosestrife

This pushy plant —
leaves coupling up woody stems,
crepe skirts swirling pink, a ballroom
where bees booze up, a rakish thirst.
This reveler of damp fields
weaving rootstock beneath a fuchsia sway.
What does it matter to such a force
that few speak highly of it?
I rave at the sight of this wild bacchanal
that saved a gray day from my indifference.

Riddled

"Why is a raven like a writing-desk?"
— Lewis Carroll

To Carroll, I reply that the ravenous
and the receptive both wait for death.
The raven picks the cat clean.
The desk is dead wood and takes dictation.

But don't mention madness.
That only scratches the surface of why
one life is another's death.
Why blood dries black on declarations of war.

How eloquence can justify murder
and invective preys on silence.
See — a feather floats down to the desk.
Quick, make the quill. Resist!

Life Is Up

Outside my window, two sparrows go at it.

I read in the paper how a car crashes into a wall.
Speed doubled, bricks collapsd, the boy's neck was broken.

In a moment it's over, a quick flutter of wings.

His bed was still warm, the pillow dented,
half-finished homework, yesterday's jeans on the floor.

The sparrows fly apart. Life is up and away.

The head-rush, the pedal pressed to the floor. Was it
the thrill before acceleration left the body behind?

A Grave Imagine

I walk the shadow
in blinding doubt.

No fault — no redemption.
No savior — annihilation.

My thinking a thin reed
of vinegar and gall.

I brood the silence
the final cadence

the never-ending
counterpoint of options.

And long like night for morning,
angles of light, a voice, another life.

Ode to Joy

After the cadence
nothing is bearable.

Beethoven hammers
down ultimates
to delay the deafening.

And we resist the liability,
persist in humming
overtures to another life.

If we knew how to hold the sway,
how the gods would envy us.

World's End Reservation

I lie in warm-scented grass amid crickets
whose wings quicken with the rising heat,
two trills per second, then four.
Ichor dances in my veins.

I forget the dead squirrel
I lifted from behind the rake.
How fur flew off
like a dandelion clock.

When cold will make the crickets stop
is not a question that interests me.
This hour I am looking for nothing
that otherwise might be.

Muse

Strike the viol, touch the lute
— Nahum Tate

The moth with folded wings
motionless on the window sill
camouflaged among ordinary things

watches the flame burning
from the lamp until
the moth with folded wings

twitches with the asking
the why of standing still
camouflaged among ordinary things

when light but briefly clings
to the wick, the ink to the quill.
The moth unfolds its wings

lifts off the ledge of being
loath, thrashes at the gilt
camouflaged among ordinary things,

willing to risk everything
willing above all to kill
the moth with folded wings
camouflaged among ordinary things.

Charles River Tango

The heron stands, a stick,
a stillness in blowsy sedge.
I steer my canoe alongside
expecting a lumbering lift-off
but she turns to pace the shore.

Elegant in her long-legged
pageant walk, she leans
into the wind, into the spotlight
of late afternoon sun,
the two of us in a slow tango.

We eye each other.
We will never part!

But I break the gaze,
the eelgrass under the boat
flickering long fingers.
I change partners as
easily as any restless heart.

Crow

I have something urgent to say but the saying
is like striking a wet match. Inside I'm raw
with trying, my spasm wit disobeying
while at my pen jabs the hungry crow.

Strings unstrung, thoughts stretched on frets,
my fingers plunk haphazard tunes,
double meanings forged and faked to death.
Crickets shrill awake the hunter's moon.

At last a music thrums and I persist
past critics in the grass. I write wringing
gist from jettison. I write 'til the sky is lit,
advancing over the stone walls, singing.

And I have fodder to feed the crow,
mineral-rich, that thing I didn't know.

Raking

They swirl faster than I
can pull them into piles.

Armful after armful
I gather and push down,
press out the last air,

crush friable spines,
inhaling musk and myrrh.

The lessening continues
above me, inexorable
the thinning, letting go

until even solitary blazes
burn cold. No different

from other falls except
I have raked up so many
and still, the dying.

Red and gold spills
inside my eyelid.

Night Walk: November

An earlier rain hangs
on a confusion of wires.
Clouds part, leaving air short
of breath, an uneasy chill on my neck.
Houses line the empty streets in uniform
indifference — closed doors, drawn curtains.
Only my feet, noisy and alive.

Leaves lie in gray vacancy beneath ice.
Unburdened, the trees prepare for winter.
Their cells shrink and sweeten to resist
freezing, teaching me to take less
space in the world. I find air in
the blue smoke of my exhale.
Relinquish, reconcile.

Nothing in Excess, Everything

A stone dog, a cross, pedestals
and so many dead —
Amy Lowell, Winslow Homer, Oliver Wendell Holmes,

the flute and furrow of their names
in principled New England granite,
hyphens incised between dates.

Nothing can subdue the precarious
iron gates, their spiked finials.
In the azaleas, bees, very much alive.

And I, a breakable thing.

The newest stones are flat.
Near Willow Pond, six fresh mounds.
Beside one, a man lies on his back,

listens to a young woman
who reads aloud and leans in
just a little.

Nothing in excess, everything
inside the sound of her voice,
his attention. Simple grieving.

There is so much less than this.

After an Early Snow

Clean-edged houses keep distance.
Fences square off vast white fields
where grass waits to prove green.
Birches, stripped, are candid
against a cobalt sky.
Even the air has teeth.

Just over the rise the sea never freezes,
ever moving in and out over land.
The marsh fills, drains, leaving
crabs and snails stranded. An egret
probes the icy cordgrass, devours
what it can before water quickens.

As with words, never a surfeit,
never certainty, only self-rationing urgency.

Speeding Past April

By New York, trees are mantled yellow and pink.
Five hours south and leaves unfold fully fledged.
We have hit the future ahead of schedule.

Returning, cars stall on the Jersey Turnpike.
And to make it worse we have been tricked
by trees that fold up flags, buds that clench fists.

Cascade Link

No water murmurs down the mountainside.
The brook, only a rumor spread by moss
brilliant with the down-pouring of another day.
A rocky bed strewn with velvet pillows
seals in, leaf by rootless leaf, that last moisture.
Down long birch boughs gold bracelets
cascade as sun breaks though the shade.
I want to lay my cheek, hot with the climb,
against this florescent fabric, imprint its mantra,
its repetition of singular plants, to find out
word by word when the stream will sing again.

Nest

It had to start somewhere.
Why not at the top
of this nearly dead pine?
Why not where branches stop
reaching and come
to a kind of crux?

It calls for something?
A few sticks and the sense
to lay them this way.
What's left is moss
to soften the inside,
bark to sharpen the rim.

Pastorales Tahitiennes

— after a painting by Paul Gaugin

The tree will not reveal itself,
roots clutch the ground,
leaves remain staunchly green.

Look long and words go,
yellow vibrates,
a pipe tune wrestles
shadows from the ground,

buds burst pink smoke,
orange flames,
a rock opens a saffron eye.

Stay long enough and see
voltaic milkweed in twilight,
hear river's black throat echo

Virgin and Vermillion gods
in their dusky pleasure.

The Compulsion of Eve

The taste I desire is more robust
than fruits sulphured by an endless serene,
a masterminded garden.

I want to see into the core,
taste the fruit I must avoid,
know how to satisfy myself.

Leave this lethargy to labor
in fields, sow my own with salt,
thresh grain from a wedge of dark.

Time Piece

A sun-bleached hayfield. At one end
a glaring green and yellow tractor.

Two minutes up field. One minute
down. I can set my watch. Instead,

I set out to watch thin spears jitter
in the mower's draft, stiffen under

spinning blades, all angles
flitching, felling. What's left lies still,

fast drying in the midday heat,
to be rolled and carted away.

The driver wears an orange cap.
His glove grabbing the stick,

shifts forward, back, forward,
back over the uneven ground.

He does not veer from his task.
A plot of land that won't be hurried.

A measure of time amazed
because I am watching.

Nik Wallenda Walks a Wire
Across Niagara Falls

Into a theater of wind and mist
a cable dips, disappears.

He moves steadily,
    each step shortening
        the improbable.
            He dissolves into thunder.

The camera loses   then finds his face
soaked, focused
on distance relenting.

In shoes his mother made
elk-skin suede
his feet curl along the wire.

He tells the cameraman
    his arms are numb.
        Weighs the long pole
            in sighs, side to side.

And we can see
    the waters waiting
        the letting go
            the urge to.

He inches ahead
    each second of inertia
        a pinpoint
            from which we too
                step forward.

The Fallacy of Four Terms

Nothing is better than eternal happiness.
A ham sandwich is better than nothing.
Therefore, a ham sandwich is better than eternal happiness.

Insects in amber caught upon a time once
climbing as if it mattered, no end in sight.
If I scratch the line *no end in sight* it still ends.

The fastening of wings. No flight. Nothing
everlasting. Even being, a bluff
over the abyss. No matter.

Make time for once upon knowing.
Taste the host or host a tavern brawl.
Dance a half-assed tango into the Red Bliss of potatoes.

A good lunch is better than immortality.

From the Next Galaxy

I appear suddenly, a new luminosity —
my adolescent flares, aura, my hot core,
a stellar performance. Off-kilter
I spin a final settling in.
I am fire finding its axis.

To become spent passion, particulate —
love faking, mad money making,
a bride of three times?
Oxygen and bitter sulfur
fused cold, my heart inert?

Or hurl through space
a silver cast! All my selves
unhinged from hurt.